OH THERE YOU ARE I CAN'T SEE YOU IS IT RAINING?

LAURA BROADBENT

Edited by Darren Wershler
Designed by Jon Paul Fiorentino

Library and Archives Canada Cataloguing in Publication

Broadbent, Laura
Oh there you are I can't see you is it raining / Laura Broadbent.

Poems.
ISBN 978-0-9865765-9-1

I. Title.

PS8603.R61O58 2012 C811'.6 C2012-905438-0

Printed and bound in Canada.
Represented in Canada by Literary Press Group
Ditributed by LitDistCo
SNARE BOOKS
4832A Parc Avenue
Montreal, QC
H2V 4E6
snarebooks.wordpress.com

OH THERE YOU ARE I CAN'T SEE YOU IS IT RAINING?

LAURA BROADBENT

SNARE

"I'll lie down and take you in my arms. I'll roll with you in the midst of great secrets. We'll lose ourselves, and find ourselves again. Nothing will come between us any more. How unfortunate that you won't be present for this happiness!"

– Maurice Blanchot

BETWEEN

A

AND

B

"Language is encrusted upon the living"
– Henri Bergson

A.

What of the space between A and B. Zeno suggests infinity. Quantum Zeno: the dynamic evolution (motion) of a quantum system can be hindered (or inhibited) through observation of the system. In other words your observation inhibits my dynamic evolution. In other words it is important to be alone. Observation incites opinion, opinion encourages names, names are made of language and language is made of chains.

B.

A.

A was her home; B was her school. At A they appointed her with multiple names at B they appointed her with multiple names. Did she ask for these names? All these names don't get it. They don't get it and she can't say it. So in the space between, she walked and looked and breathed and smelled until she was nothing but a staring problem nothing but a nostril. She called this space perfect this space between A and B, this space between two places that slapped names upon her and between two places upon which she slapped names. What violence, this naming. While walking she abandoned them.

B.

A.

The anxiety of place beckons persona. Shed whenever possible. The cadence of vanishing. Certain things occur when language is abandoned. There are no eyes to inhibit. Space takes on shimmer and fortissimo. The fact of its bigness makes one borderless. Language has limits, language is linear, made of chains.

B.

A.

Your task is to smell the morning and there's nothing wrong with what you're wearing and your hair's just fine so notice the wild staccato and sinew of sound from the loud to minute brush of dry grass there is no violence or direction let's say it's lightly snowing and every snowflake has the power of an extraterrestrial crystal palace of monumental healing and light so who cares if your decisions have been correct. No you, no you, no you.

B.

A.

Even your family can betray you but when there is no you your family can't betray you. The place between A and B formally requests you drop the story. He is not better than you because there is no you and you have not failed because there is no you. You did not say the wrong thing because there is no you. There was no humiliating sexual encounter because there is no you. You didn't detect bodily decay because there is no you. He cannot hurt you because there is no you. You aren't stuck in your first-world issues because there is no you. Your task is to walk among the ten thousand things - look at the sky and become it smell the morning and become it feel the temperature and become it scatter with the wind. Not a name reaches you in your bassinet of nothingness strung between A and B.

B.

A.

One is so layered. The sky is vast and will relieve each layer you release. Each turns into a fine mist that lifts. This is who you are, so they say, now let it go. Now this is who you are, so they say, now let it go. Now this is who you are, so they say, now let it go. Now this is who you are, so they say, now let it go. And finally what's left but the gentle breath. And who says this bitch is anything but gentle let it go what they say let it go in the space between two places, it will take it and you will see it was all nothing and by that I mean everything. In this space you aren't forgiven because there is no you to forgive so in that sense you are forgiven. You can practice this in jail. It's very nice, it's very stylish.

B.

A.

You and every annoying song you ever heard, just a wave, baby, just a wave. Don't worry you're a great dancer.

B.

A.

In between is not uninteresting. Trying to be interesting is not interesting. What destroys mediocrity, sensitivity destroys mediocrity, that's what destroys mediocrity. Animals have awareness radically different than our own. This animal can fly and this animal can see in the dark and licks his own eyeballs and this animal has electromagnetic compasses in its eyeballs and what was it you were saying about being interesting? If you are nothing then no names stick. To be nothing is to say I am not my face but without saying it, just being faceless. The best thing about you nobody can see anyway so you might as well go out in the blue ocean in a blue boat and wear your finest blue suit oh yes there you are I can't see you. Is it raining?

B.

CULLED

SUITE 1

"Obviously the soul of each is longing for something else which it cannot put into normal words but keeps trying to express in oracles and riddles."

– Plato, Symposium

[1]
And all our ladies
humbled by the significance
of stifling insanity
and constant birth.
Only the voice of
turquoise monuments.

[2]
Chorus the dawn swan dance sun.
Do these cupcakes make me human?
The doctor was astounded!
I quite liked the taste of them.
You turkey wing, don't start waitressing.

[3]
Ten times in the chest but still whistling.
The reason you're hurting is because of the cupcake.
I once met an old black queen who said
'Know how you flow,
fill in the blank with a friend's name,
forget about the moon -
she's just a drunk kid, hours after her curfew.'

[4]
Here lies my account of
black balloons of thoughts
which I blame on my menstruation
(and that's three cupcakes now).

[5]
The sun is shining and we are all stupid
with the capacity for delicate perversions.
All in the enormous theatre crying very hard.
When four sides are at arms and legs length,
you know exactly where not to go.

[6]
Any distraction will do.
Life was already drowning her
but too slowly.
My meltdown indicates being more social.
‘Beautiful! Beautiful!’
‘Damn right.’

[7]
Enjoy a panoramic view of a brick wall.
The ancient consolation:
Let Bell notify you when the line becomes available.

[8]
Waiting for the system configurations
I examine a bug that landed on my breast.
Everything's an earthquake,
these salt-shaker days.

[9]
If there is no wind, be one with the insects.
Love between women is a refuge.

[10]
The man thought I had a lazy eye!
A boy's got urges, you know?
I'm in a Russian novel:
vertiginous ascents and descents.

[11]
Stifling insanity
and constant birth.
If there is no wind,
be one with the insects.

[12]
I'm in a Russian novel
(which I blame on my menstruation).
The ancient consolation:
any distraction will do.

[13]
Do these cupcakes make me human?
Shining with the capacity
for delicate perversions?
The doctor was astounded.

[14]
Enjoy a panoramic view of
a bug that landed on my breast:

15]
Here lies my account of
constant birth.
‘Beautiful! Beautiful!’
‘Damn right.’

[16]
Vertiginous ascents and descents
and that's three cupcakes now.

[17]
You know exactly where not to go.
Humbled by the significance.

[18]
A boy’s got urges, you know?
A panoramic view of
a drunk kid, hours after her curfew.

[19]
Life was already drowning her
but too slowly.
Let Bell notify you when the line becomes available.

[20]
Because of the cupcake.

SUITE 2

"Repeating then is in every one, in every one their being and their feeling and their way of realizing everything and every one comes out of them in repeating."

– Gertrude Stein

[1]
Some fruits, vegetables, and grains.
A peaceful bore,
idle but occupied.
There's an aesthetics to wasting time
and this is no exaggeration.

[2]
No exaggeration:
messy love is better than none
since we can't fart around pretty things
and our decay never ceases to disappoint.
These are the manifestations of faith.

[3]
Faith:
If a star is in the process of exploding
its misery makes it special.

[4]
Maybe they think their misery makes them special.
'Miraculous' and 'mercy'
assumes a depth
but in Canada
it's all well-to-do and somewhat boring
i.e Fuck it I just want to cuddle.

[5]
Fuck it,
I do not love as much as I used to
so now I can be like a regular person
just warm the quiche, the coffee
while being a devastation zone.

[6]
Being a devastation zone
I doubt will kill me, it will just feel like death.
It's useless to demand meaning or resolution
in the face of such a yawning abyss.
Am I right or am I right?

[7]
Am I right:
Be modest and correct.
The inevitable blows of coexisting with others
also bring us closer (for now).
Well. Isn't this just all massively harmonious.

[8]
Massively harmonious,
deeply stupidly restful and indulgent.
My grand opus is
romance: the great time-waster.
Resolution: asexuality and personal indifference.

[9]
Asexuality and personal indifference
are powerful personal weapons.
Biological urges serve
to make them rapt with attention.
Where is the perfectly timed kindness?
Your child will grow to be a confused asshole.

[10]
Mom, your child has grown into a confused asshole.
I am known for hysterics.
Sometimes it is sweet to be mad:
'A man sound in mind knocks in vain at the doors of poetry.'
Mostly it's my mind.

[11]
Mostly it's my mind.
Be modest and correct.
Better to be well-to-do and somewhat boring.
i.e Fuck it I just want to cuddle.

[12]
Fuck it, I just want to cuddle
(being a devastation zone).
Where is the perfectly timed kindness?
The inevitable blows of coexisting with others
I doubt will kill me. It will just feel like death.

[13]
I doubt it will kill me.
A star is in the process of exploding
assumes a depth.

[14]
Assume a depth.
In the face of such a yawning abyss
just warm the quiche, prepare the coffee.

[15]
Just warm the quiche, prepare the coffee:
these are the manifestations of faith.
My grand opus:
It's useless to demand meaning or resolution.

[16]
It's useless to demand meaning or resolution.
Fruits, vegetables, and grains
are powerful personal weapons.

[17]
A personal weapon
in the face of such a yawning abyss:
perfectly timed kindness.

[18]
Perfectly timed kindness
bring us closer (for now)
and this is no exaggeration.

SUITE 3

"All life on earth (and by extension, technology) is built upon appropriation and reuse of the preexisting."

– David Shields

[1]
Supple with incoherence, I have not
learned how to people myself.
Above all, lose any hope.

[2]
I've never enjoyed a party in my life.
This hits a little too deep.
The only women for me live a tonal complexity.

[3]
The biggest fact about anyone is their mother.
I know this is getting a little complicated.

[4]
Art school students love art school students.
There is something unutterably terrible
About art school students.

[5]
He likes it when my nails are short and clean.
Since it's love there's nothing easy about it
so I threw my wine glass at him.
Old wounds and their flatulence.

[6]
No one told me it was problematic to be a woman
until I started getting treated like one.
I Googled 'Why are all Aquarius men jerks?'
I wasn't the first.

[7]
When I try to describe you
my mouth gets an E for Effort.
I invite you for a dip and you think
its an invitation to drowning.
Find some bearings
then ostensibly learn to keep them.

[8]
Obligatory fun is ostensible fun.
The project of the intellectuals.
Don't open an intellectual
unless you want to be killed.

[9]
To lose those I love most.
What other lessons are there –
how to make a perfect gazpacho?
I still believe in forces.

[10]
Anger is one of my charming knacks.
Also panic for no discernible reason.
I remember things with my whole body.
Men like it when I ostensibly behave.

[11]
Supple with incoherence
Art school students are
terrible
at making the perfect
gazpacho.

[12]
Obligatory fun gets an E
for Effort. When you've lost
those you love most,
your only hope is in
charming pastimes.

[13]
The biggest fact is a little complicated.
Throw your wine glass at it
then clean your nails and Google
'ostensible women.'

[14]
I invited you for a dip
then you treat me like a woman.
Google: 'old wounds
AND tonal complexity.'

[15]
Getting killed: obligatory fun.
No need to get all emotional
and intellectual about it.

[16]
The project of the intellectuals:
the terrible fact of
women and flatulence.

[17]
Everyone's mother is problematic
trying to do something about
feeling unloved.

[18]
Art school students' projects are parties.
Be on guard for the projects of art students.

[19]
Men like when my whole body
is ostensible.

[20]
Remembering things
is an invitation to drowning.

MEN IN VARIOUS STATES

"It's you I'm scared of and your penis,
That menace to good boys and bad."

– Catullus

I.

Month 1.
Julia is a true artist.
Every man she's wounded,
She's wounded in a new way.

Month 2.
It's been one of those days. A variation of every day and on this particular day I sit on the toilet in the arts building, working on easing a runny shit out of my stomach made murky by a strange sandwich and two cups of black coffee and I'm sitting there feeling tired even though the day has only begun, thinking, not thinking, just feeling how sad I am, how deeply sad and jealous and angry and full of hate and how tired I am from my own mind looping like a sick fly at a windowsill and I think about the dude painting the mural downstairs, how good it is, how handsome he is, how unattractive I am, how Julia probably dreams of being with him if she is not yet with him, how he's the good I'll never be, how my mind is bent from being abandoned by Julia, and WHAT and WHO can I believe in after that when the automatic industrial-powered toilet begins flushing because I shifted around a little, so I have to stand up with my pants down, unwiped, so the toilet will not suck my organs out of my asshole, then I sit back down and feel like crying, and I think I better move in with my parents for a year, I better wave the flag of defeat be-

cause I am an exposed nervous system giving off sparks, I want to cry all the time, I use all my strength to get out of bed and the only thing I look forward to is getting back in, and I'm too thick, and this is how it feels, all very indulgent and you're probably thinking Get a Grip, Buddy, and that actually feels good because you are confirming that I am a piece of shit and whatever I have no shame.

Month 3.
I have visions about doing things I would not actually do. Things that you are taught definitely not to do. For example I imagine punching her so that her nose bleeds but is not broken, throwing her to the ground, kicking her thigh but not her stomach because there are limits, pulling her hair, straddling her and slapping her over and over across the face with a fly swatter. As she lies there crying, I tell her, 'I am doing this because I feel really bad.'

II.

I am the sort of man women say they love
but never recognize when they meet me
and even if they did recognize me
they wouldn't recognize me.
Because I am the sort of man
women say they love but would never
recognize when they meet me because
they want to "want to" meet me,
not actually meet me.
For if they met me, the sort of man
women say they love, they wouldn't
love me, for I am precisely the man
that they say they love and do
not actually love.

I am the sort of man who endures
the sensitivity of his feelings.

Since I am the sort of man women say they love
but never recognize when they meet me
then I am just a man with potential
for being loved, and not the sort of man
who is loved.
Any wide space of ground is the potential

site of a palace but there is no palace
until the palace is built.
To be loved consists in being loved
not having the potential
for being loved.
So if I am to be a man women actually love
rather than the sort of man women say
they love but never recognize when they
meet me, I need to be the sort of man
women say they don't love, for then
I will be loved.

III.

Ella thought it was time we spiced up our marriage. "Okay," I said, but "Impossible," I thought. I thought she would have forgotten about it by evening but when I got home from work she said, "massage lessons!" I saw she had been waiting all day to say that. Again, she said, "spice up our marriage." I took a moment to appraise my wife and said to her in my head, "Ella I am the most wretched man alive if you haven't noticed and the lights in your eyes that are massage lessons that will spice up our marriage makes me a wretched AND unbearably sad man and you know and I know very well nothing's going to work, nothing's going to work, not ever." She continued to smile and the white immaculate kitchen behind her appeared to be smiling in the same manner. "Okay," I said to her instead, "Sure," and turned to the bathroom to blink away the tears.

The first night of class was a tutorial for the men, or as the instructor put it, for the more yang-identified. It was an enormous class. This filled me with a philanthropic sadness because I realized I wasn't the only one with a yin-identified half that thought her marriage needed spicing up. The men and women were ushered into separate rooms, the women clutching white towels. They were to change out of their clothes and return to the massage tables, lie on their stomachs, and cover their bums with the towels. "Okay significant others!" the instructor called out, "Okay, significant others, come on out now, your partners are ready to receive as you learn to channel healing into transformative love." We, the significant others, had been standing behind the door, saying nothing. I was used to this however, because I rode the elevator to and from the eleventh floor at work five days a week. During this awkward intermission I noticed that one of the significant others may or may not have been a woman so I looked down in search of breasts and I looked up to see daggers. I said in my mind to this woman who was for sure a woman, "Sorry." If she only knew I care nothing for breasts. I have tried, I pretend, but I do not care for sloppy udders. That's when the instructor called out and one of the significant others opened the door. He may or may not have been a childhood friend – cute, too.

There were over thirty beds in that room, each one containing a woman, her bum made bulbous by the white towel. Two things occurred to me. The first was that all the bums reminded me of the balls of dough I would poke as a child, the steaming, kneaded, flesh-toned dough my mother would cover with a towel to let rise. The second thing I noticed made my heart start racing in a way it had not raced since I was eleven and about to jump of the highest diving board at the Quarry (despite my paralyzing fear of heights, might I add): I didn't know which woman was my wife. They all could have been Ella, or none of them. Faces down, all various stages of risen dough. Their bums were so outrageous, so globulous, nothing like the deliciously tight, tidy, sculpted mounds of men. I had no inclination to find her. This was my chance to turn, sprint in the opposite direction, and never look back. Exhilarating, blinding, deafening. I heard music in my ears that I wanted to make more than sex, and MUCH more than babies. I was going to make music in my free time, make music forever. No wife, just guitar, drums, tablas, kora, harp, steel drums, shakuhatchi, erhu, dulcimer, bass, cello, piano. I was going to learn to record and engineer, and I was going to do nothing but, until I died: punk rock, post rock, art rock, rock rock, jazz, death metal, freak folk, experimental, hip hop, doo wop, klezmer, reggae jazz funk fusion, and classical. I'll invite that boy who leads the St. James choir.

"Sir," called the teacher from the front of the room, "Sir," she called again. All the mates had significant others but one. I could hear my heart in my ears, feel it in my balls. I inched toward this woman. A boy on the high dive carefully turning around to make a slow march back to the ladder, and a shaky descent.

IV.

Sit Across From Your Partner And Close Your Eyes. Synchronize Your Breath. Move To The Center Of The Darkness. Your Partner Will Ask, 'Who Are You?' And You Will Answer Each Time With The First Image That Comes To Your Mind. Continue This Rhythm Until I Sound The Tibetan Bowl.

Who are you?
I am a dog catching a ball. I am a dog bringing the ball back to the thrower. I am a dog waiting for the ball to be thrown again.
Who are you?
I am a burrito.
Who are you?
I am a crisis.
Who are you?
I am a discarded plastic duck in the middle of the Pacific, rising with the waves, falling with the waves, never being pushed to shore.
Who are you?
More than that which the idealist calls a representation, but less than that which the realist calls a thing.
Who are you?
I am matter and memory.
Who are you?
Not you.

Who are you?
I am a cloud. A data cloud.
Who are you?
I am a paper trail.
Who are you?
I am a Screech Owl with sharp talons and a mournful wavering trill.
Who are you?

[Tibetan Bowl]

V.

Dreams about Erin since I left her:

I.
Unseen, watching her walk in the snow. I get to love her the way I did before the things that couldn't be forgotten. The little wisps of hair at her temples ruffling with the wind.

II.
She climbs onto my back at night and bites, leaving a big painful hole. It really hurts. She is whispering stuff in my ear and licking it.

III.
My family moves into this enormous airplane hangar in the sky that's been renovated into castle art gallery playhouse thing, and also a restaurant. All the ceilings are really high, at least 30 feet. My bedroom has this hazy white glow to it, and there's a window high up. There's a bassinette in my room also which freaks me out because it's me as a baby inside. My family calls me to dinner and I say I'll meet them shortly. I'm feeling really sad so much so that it's hard to move. I walk around a corner dragging my feet and its Erin. Her presence in this airplane hangar place is unbelievable, joyous. I ask if she is going to stay, terrified that she isn't. Terrified. But she was! So then she took me through the museum

part of the building she was curating. I kept on trying to hump her.

VI.

How was I to know that after I married Helen, I would meet Lee?
How was I to know that when I married Lee, I would meet Leah?
How was I to know?

VII.

Home could be in the rectum of Alberta but it is special. Home is not special in and of itself, but becomes special through a process. Home is a place you once had never known; you grow and move around it until you know its name and all its contours, until you call its name with confidence. This place dims the cacophony of the outside. Intimacy with increased intensity. When you leave, the idea of it elicits a yearning. As with a lover.

This yearning must be kept as a yearning: it is always better to imagine these lost lovers than to experience them. I remember that Drew is dull as dishwater, but I imagine Drew as Adonis.

To lose one's home. Rarely does this mean one's home has become a parking lot. Often the home is still there, but some circumstance restricts return. It's the most banal state of desire. Hear stories of others who may visit it, but be unable, yourself, to ever go back.

I'm getting to this. The man you love, after years, becomes home. And to lose the man is to lose your home all over again. To lose the man you love means he is still there, you hear about him, hear stories from others who may visit him, but you are unable to ever go back. Worse to lose him while he's still there.

VIII.

February 14, 2011

Dear Mr. Baxter.

Hello, it is me, your Valentine of the year 2011. I am pleased to be occupying this position, though the job has not been without cataclysmic and paralyzing setbacks. However, one thing I have learned in my time here is that love need not be so cataclysmic and paralyzing. Also, I'm getting too old for that shit.

In writing this missive I am intimidated by the possibilities of style: what would please you (as I do so want to excel at this job) most? Would you like something cryptic and abstract with strange spelling, arcane diction, square brackets, ellipses? Would you like something poetic and transcendent and mystical? Would you like something dirty and raunchy, something that causes stirrings in your groin? Or should I keep it professional?

Speaking candidly, I would like to confront one of the many ironies of contemporary living, wherein two people may act professionally despite the fact that they have seen each other naked, smelled each other naked, sucked each other naked, licked each other naked, and slept together naked, not to mention that they have lived together in a domestic atmosphere. They have fought righteously. Hammond has broken a table, infringed upon Chad's email privacy two times, and fired him; Chad has spit on Hammond, kicked him, punched him, swore at him, screamed at him, broken a glass at his feet, drooled, beaten his own head with his own hands, and smashed his head against a wall in utter savage frustration. They have fucked in washrooms, outside on the rocks by a river, in a tree, on a bunk bed, their office, in Chad's laundry room, at his new house, on Hammond's couch, in his kitchen, on the floor, and sometimes in bed. Isn't it strange that two people who have collaborated so intimately can still work together on a professional basis to organize an event for the day of St. Valentine? Is that healthy?

Still speaking candidly, (or perhaps I am taking this too far) I want to say that I hope you don't fire me again. Or if you fire me, you move your business away from the neighborhood so that we do not repeat our failed attempts at a harmonious partnership. In other words, fuck me or fire me, Mr. Baxter – but do it lovingly. Regardless of the outcome, what I can say is that though our business may be shaky, it has real heart and soul. I know those two words do not fare well in the business world, but one cannot kill their inner poet completely.

I thought, because of this romantic day, that I would list the things about you that I adore. However, it is my belief that I do that enough, if not far too often, and I'm sure you would agree. No, I should not. Nor will I apologize for my suspiciousness and jealousy, my inimical rage, my mercurial nature, my poverty, or my wandering eye, as these are part in parcel of what makes up your most fantastic employee. Sometimes you want to fire me, I know, while other times you want to promote me to CEO. Regardless of your judgment and lapses in patience and vision, rest assured you could not find a better business partner, one with true grit and gristle. It's a give and take. Plenty of times I would like to have fired you, if I could, but I can't. So no, it's not a give-and-take, never mind. I do not have it in me to abandon this project, or you, and so you must give me a raise.

To be honest, partaking in this business was a leap of faith. I had just emerged from the wreckage of a previous failed business expenditure; I knew what I was in for. But there was something in your authentic, refined and calm style that made me a believer. To begin a business in mutual poverty is never a good idea, and you certainly aren't large and in charge when it comes to PR. And neither am I. Good thing we have our cat. To be fair, I realize one big reason I got the job is that I hid from you the extremes to which my previous business ventures failed. We all downplay the truth behind our suits, no?

In keeping this position I intend to approach it with stubborn persistence and proverbial patience and, regardless of its final success, I intend to derive as much of an education from it, and you, as possible. It won't be now, it won't be in a year, but in many years, we could even have a puppy. I like to think big. On the other hand, I keep the possibility of this partnership caving always in the back of my mind, as ventures to which I have given grit and marrow have fallen through before (as we already know far, far too well). I know very well and at all times that this failure is a possibility, and that I could get fired any time (as you have shown me in the past – fuck you, but also thank you for giving me a second and fourteenth chance) so I try not to get too attached and remember that impermanence lies at the heart of all things. There are many other business options out there. And if you fire me again, I must say, it is your loss. I have enormous muscles.

IX.

There is a park and there is an I in the park.
There is a mound in the park and there are people in the park.
The park people walk behind the mound.
There is a park and there is a mound and there are women throwing a Frisbee.
The women throw and walk and smile before they are swallowed by the mound.
There is a park with a mound, with me, with women with Frisbees.

I am beneath an old tree, in the park with the mound, half watching the women
before they are swallowed.
There are many trees, all of which, I forgot to mention, are old
in this park of women and mounds.
There is a tree in front of me that the sunset has chosen –
it is neither happy nor sad but surely illuminated.
I have chosen the tree that was not chosen by the sunset so I accept
the big ants crawling down my shirt because of my choice.
It is not the ant but my relationship to the ant: so, ant, you are not a soldier
with six legs and no emotions, you are merely ticklish.
I do not expect this old tree to mend my heart or loneliness

nor do I expect it to teach me anything.
It doesn't care if I look up at it, and look at up it, and keep on looking up at it.
so I do not stop looking up at it.
Nor does the mound care as I keep on looking at the mound
as it swallows the women.
I cannot name the types of birds singing nor the types of ants that navigate my flesh
and I do not blame the ants for navigating my flesh.

There is a park and I am in the park with the mound and the passing women who disappear behind the mound and there are the ants and there are old trees beneath which I sit with my heart that I do not expect the trees to mend. There is the hum of night and I will not not look up at the tree and at the mound that swallows the women and I will not stop the ants from navigating my flesh and there is this beer I didn't mention the beer.

X.

I say, only bored and privileged girls get to say what you say. She says nothing she slaps me she cries she phones her girlfriend she's silent for days. Life is tenuous As. It. Is. Why would I make it all the more dangerous by taking emotional risks and 'loving dangerously,' whatever that even means. Monogamy is an enormous risk, and now she wants more risk. Suicidal homicidal 'loving dangerously.' All Shakespearian characters have mental problems. There are times I am sure she is unstable. Always haranguing for explanations and answers. Haranguing for explanations and answers will never get you explanations or answers. Especially if they are to questions that I do not even think about in the first place. She is always wanting to make plans. Not to take emotional risks or for love to be unsafe or to have endless plans, no - what she wants is to grind.

XI.

He says that she says that he said something he didn't say.
She says that he says that she said something she didn't say.
He says she says things when she means something else.
She says he says mean things.

He says she says he says mean things
and he says he does not say mean things.
He says he says things that mean something
and he says she says things
that don't mean anything.

She says she can't believe he says she says
things that don't mean anything
and that he says he says things
that mean something because
what he actually says, she says,
are mean things that mean mean things.

He says she can say he says mean things
only if she lists the mean things he says
and if she can't list the mean things he says
then he simply says things that mean things.

She says precisely because he says she must list
the mean things means he says mean things.
She says she can't list the mean things he means
because she says he says she only says things
that don't mean anything and she says that
if she says things that don't mean anything
at least she says things that don't mean anything
rather than saying things that mean mean things.

He says he's sorry she thinks he says things
that mean mean things and that maybe she
shouldn't invest such meaning in the things
he means because he doesn't mean them.
He says that yes sometimes he says things
that mean mean things just to be mean.
He says for example he doesn't mean it
when he says she says things that don't mean
anything or mean something else, he is just
saying those things to be mean.

She says that what he says no longer
has any meaning no matter how mean
and she says she's not sure they've said
anything that means anything anyway
so perhaps they should stop saying things
and just make coffee to which he agrees.

XII.

She looked over to me looking at her and said I need a fire ceremony to burn all my old love letters. I told her that could be arranged. I told her I've burnt all the love letters I've ever received. Except for hers. Which will probably get burned one day too, she says. I told her, probably, but so will my corpse. She laughed without smiling.

XIII.

Do not grow old. I assure you I would have killed myself long ago if a stupid curiosity and my own laziness had not prevented a timelier exit. When you are an old man, when you are on talking terms with all the tortures of the soul and of the body, you reach a void of which you are terribly conscious. You see things that cannot touch you, and you see things you cannot touch. And you can't hear for shit. You have been too dulled to be consoled. You do not care enough to care, yet you are aware that you cannot care, and this awareness makes you sad. Stuck in a mason jar with very little oxygen left and you don't care enough to finish thinking about –

Have you ever seen an old man's penis? There is a reason for that.

XIV.

I watch things happen to her, and I enjoy watching things happen to her.
I watch her go out with These People for This Night.
To her the people are important, the night is an event.
To her, These People: all, This Night: everything.

I watch her prepare, I watch her change and re-change her clothes.
I listen to her fret, to her opine about these people.
I watch her participate.
A loud night, a dark room full of indistinct faces except the few distinct faces,
who are These People about whom I have listened to her speak.

I watch her get drunk and gelatinous, cheeks streaked with makeup.
One of the People made her cry.
I hold her. I enjoy her as she cries.
I watch her pass out on the bed.
She mumbles sweet things to me.
I like when she mumbles.
She tries to kiss me and burps.
I enjoy that, too.

I watch her confront the next morning.
I listen to her speak on her cell.
  Sing-songy, her "I don't know" a perfect "Me-Ray-Doe".
  There is music to the sound of her need to chat.

I look to see if The Night has changed her. There is no sign.
I like watching things happen to her. She likes to have things happen to her.
  The flurry of activity appears to just flow right through her.
  She takes it in, remains unchanged.

A child is trying to put two blocks in her bucket.
She bends to grab the red block, puts it away, but the blue block tips out
She bends to pick up the blue block, puts it away, but the red block tips out
She doesn't seem to know there are only two blocks. Or doesn't care.
Just the picking up and the putting away.

XV.

My extent of knowledge about women is as follows:
1: “Watch your tone of voice.”
2. “I am irrational and a little bit crazy.”
3. “Don’t ever live with me.”
4. “You will never understand me, ever.”

XVI.

Everything wet
is attached to emotion.

Fingering won't keep
her.

A meeting is
accidental, routine.

She'll own you
as insurance against decay.

Girls bloom perennial.

XVII.

Borges says to fall in love is to create a religion that has a fallible god. Marcus says that for as long as he's known me – that is eight years – I have either been in a relationship or recovering from one.

I know now that I have never invented a feeling, that there is nothing I have ever felt that has not been felt by others before and perhaps at the same time as me. I know this because I have read this, and I have felt this before I read this, and I have felt this after I have read this. I am not alone, as lonely as I am and this is discouraging though it is supposed to be encouraging. My reading confirms this.

Marcus tells me that what I need is to just casually date girls. I have never done that, and I do not think I can change, though I can only imagine how lightly they step upon the earth, Those Who Just Casually Date. I can imagine that their chests are not crushed daily, multiple times, when overcome by the memory of kissing the feet of a God who has abandoned them.

Diana is a babe from Sarnia who can play guitar. Jenny is a confused scared girl with a great work ethic from B.C. Chloe is a metaphysical thinker from Stratford who can make a perfect omelet. I forget and call each one God. And they still are and they still aren't and I think there is just residue from my religious childhood aching that places God in the pussy and promises of some confused girl who is also God. I tell myself She is just a confused girl from [...] to comfort myself, but I also know she is God. I have read this and I have also seen this and I have felt this.

Everyone calls me intense and I want to say well life is everything at once and that is intense but I don't say it. I don't know why other people aren't as intense, I always assume they are just secretly, or they have special diffusing enzymes in their systems. Sometimes I think I would not be so alone if I moved to Latin America or to certain Eastern European countries where people spank other people's children and scream because they love so much that's just what happens. As far as I can tell, though I know we are all lying to ourselves all the time, when I love someone I love with density and focus and when we split, all that pressure detonates. Harm is done. So what, stop gossiping.

Matthew says that what I need is to just move on and know my worth and not prostrate myself at the feet of a girl who is stupid enough to leave me. Zsofia says what I need is a therapist. Erin says what I need is to move back to Ontario. Luc says I need to go teach in Korea. Ryan says I need some Wild Turkey. In the course of a day, it occurs to me that I need this, yes I need this, period, or, later, I need that, yes, I need that. Period. But no solution alters the fact that I am staggered multiple times each day by a memory of Her so profound that I feel religious fervor and I must excuse myself to weep and feel profound. Nobody can see it, but it keeps me separate, I cannot let it go. I nurse it. Knowing and knowing are different things. Mom says stop being a walking battle ground. Thom says lighten the fuck up, will you. This is all very good advice.

XVIII.

Found in a box on Marcus Garvey Boulevard, Brooklyn, 2009

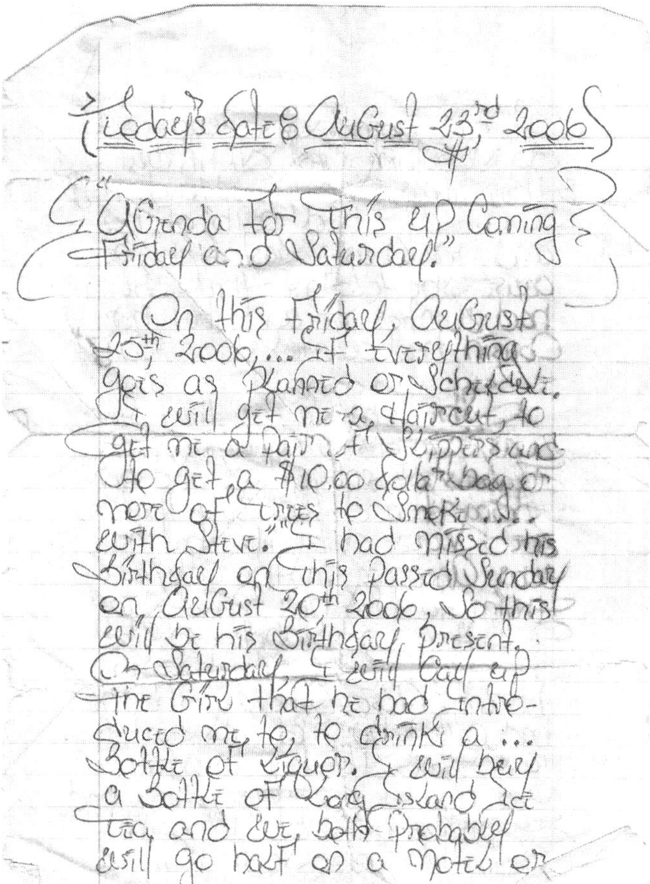
(Today's Date: August 23rd, 2006)

"Agenda For This Up Coming Friday and Saturday."

On this Friday, August 25th, 2006,... If everything goes as Planned or Scheduled. I will get me a Haircut, to get me a Pair of Slippers and to get a $10.00 dollar bag or more of "weed" to Smoke... with Steve." I had missed his Birthday on this passed Sunday on August 20th 2006, So this will be his Birthday Present. On Saturday, I will Call up the Girl that he had intro-duced me to, to drink a ... Bottle of Liquor. I will buy a Bottle of Long Island Ice Tea, and we, both Probably will go half on a Motel or

at her house." "She wanted to
do something last night, but
"there was no place to do it!"
I could've had both, of her
and her cousin last night, be-
cause she told me that she
had wanted me and that her
cousin had wanted some too!"

She was saying that Steve
was "jealous & annoying, ...
jealous of me of me and her
doing it and the way that
we were doing it. That he
was annoying in the cab/taxi
trying to feel her "privates" top
& bottom and in between that
the cab/taxi driver had to in-
tervene. Also annoying that he
had called her job at least 3
to 4 times for her to come
over his mother house, ... He had
jeopardize her job doing that,
calling her there so much."

XIX.

I think of elevators
I don't want to know
what makes them work and why,
I just want them to fulfill their function.

XX.

February 14, 1984
If Woman
existed,
you'd be
a beautiful
Woman.

February 14, 2011
Other women
exist,
but you are
the most
beautiful
Woman.

XXI.

You step onto your back porch late on a summer night and you think something when you didn't expect to think anything. You think, "Shit's been said and done" and you're untroubled with that.

You interject. "No, shit things will continue to be said, and shit things will continue to be done," and you think, "I have comprehensively said shit things and done shit things that are irrevocably said and irrevocably done," which are of course the mistakes which constitute the majority of your lived time.

A small and amiable wind lifts from nowhere. It breathes into you and you feel it lift your spirits as it would an errant dry leaf and, for a second, for less than a second, you feel all time and you fully comprehend the general largeness and, for a moment it revives you.

You keep sitting on your back porch, staring - the point being just so sit and stare and oxidize, and you realize, with all said and done as far as you're concerned, all that is left for you is inexplicable split-second moments that punctuate month-long buzzing stretches of sterility. "Fine," you think, "That's fine with me."

Acknowledgements

Mom, Dad, Uncle Michael, Stephen Welch - life support. Love.
Illingworth family – the magic of yourselves and for Gail.
Marina and Mira – meow.
Ken Mavor – early affirmation.
Mary di Michele – kind steady mentor, fighter for the economy of the soul.
Sina Queyras – toughly forced me further, hired, inspired.
Alan Bourassa – all encouragement amidst dark echelons.
Darren Wershler – wicked prof, wicked editor.
Jon Paul Fiorentino – mover, shaker.
Jordan Robson Cramer – found.
C.R.I, J.D.H, D.H.B – most intense extra-curricular education making for multiple phoenixings, love and its opposite.
Brother Matt – same as above, but more time-intensive and blood boiled.
Valdis – steady selfless brave and big-brained.
Yaniya, Allison & Deanna, Alex & Andy & Ryan -writers, fighters, bros.
The animals.
Myriade.

In Memory of Robert Kroetsch.